MW01709925

What To Feed A Vegan

James W. C. Perry

Copyright

Publisher: The Vegan Gorilla

Photographer: James Perry

Photographer: In Your Face Photography (head shot back cover)

Table Of Contents

Dedication

This book is dedicated to my family and friends who supported me these past five years.

Although I admit I never thought I could last and I'm sure they didn't either. A special thanks to Crystal for the continued support of confidence she has in me. My Son Ryan for starting me on this crazy journey when you talked to me about your school movie Forks Over Knives. Also my Son Cole for being my guinea pig and always being optimistic about trying my recipes. I wouldn't be where I am today without you all.

P.S. Also To Cousin Pete. One can never forget Cousin Pete!

Much Luv

The Vegan Gorilla

About The Author

Hello everyone.

My name is James and I would like to give you a little insight on how I founded The Vegan Gorilla.

I've been into fitness all my life and played sports growing up. I love all kinds of foods. To this day I still have a big appetite.

In my adult years I started to have issues with high cholesterol. I assumed it is genetic as some of my family members have it as well. I also developed gout in my feet in my early 20's. It continued year after year and then up to 2-3 times a year. I tore my rotary cuffs a few times each in both shoulders and have bone on bone probably from doing heavy weight lifting over the years. Never had it looked at or repaired because of the "No Pain No Gain" Mentality..Ugh.

Unfortunately it came to a point where I could hardly move my shoulders without having any severe discomfort. The thought of just putting my jacket on or off made me shutter. I was told operating was the only option that could possibly help a bit but there was no guarantee. So I never did.

One day my son came home from high school and told me about a movie they watched during class. It was called Forks Over Knives. I decided to see if I could rent the movie somehow or find it online. At the time I could only find it available on Amazon. This was in November 2013 and I thought well one day it might be on TV or I could rent it.

That Christmas not even a month later one of my sisters bought the movie for me. This shocked me because neither my son or myself said a word to anyone about this. When I asked her why she bought it for me she said she wasn't sure she just thought it was something I would like. I've never expressed any interest at becoming vegan or vegetarian at all. In fact I was a big meat eater and hardly ate any vegetables. Weird or what? (I still didn't know why she thought I would like this).

I took this as a sign. A few days after Christmas I watched the documentary. It intrigued me so much I thought I'm going to "try this plant base life style". So 12:01 New Year's Day I committed myself to going vegan and have reaped the benefits ever since.

I was able to come off my cholesterol medication after 15 years since my levels were no longer high. My blood pressure came down to better than average and my shoulders are 90% pain free. I still work out 5 days a week with weights and have no issues with pain. I have not had any gout since being vegan as well.

I truly believe being vegan is a healthier way of life not to mention the lives of the animals that are slaughtered each year. I am also leaving less of a carbon foot print on this Beautiful Earth. One of the main questions I always get asked is how do you get your protein and what do you eat? (I don't understand this question because I'm over 200 pounds.) Obviously I'm getting enough.

It's simple. Look at Gorillas. Look how strong and powerful they are and they are plant based eaters. I could be wrong but it looks like they have enough protein in their diet.

I founded The Vegan Gorilla to share my story and the benefits of being Vegan. To create great recipes inspiring non vegans and current vegans to still have one of the magnificent loves of life. *Great Food*. I work hard on coming up with these recipes so you won't feel deprived from the pleasures food has to offer and to even perhaps open you up to new flavors that was yet to be discovered across your palate.

I want to show you can still enjoy great food all the while of saving animals lives and world resources. Creating for yourself the many health benefits you will gain from it.

I value education and knowledge and spent my life achieving the following amongst a few other things.

Certified Plant Base Chef

Certified Plant Base Baker

Certified Food Handler

Certified Personal Trainer

Certified Reiki Master & Teacher

Certified Real Estate Broker

I hope this book makes it a little easier for you and perhaps even enjoy some of the meals yourself.

Much Luv

The Vegan Gorilla

Section 1

ALLERGY ALERT! PLEASE READ FIRST!

Please take a moment to familiarize yourself with all the ingredients listed in this book. There are many people maybe yourself included that are very allergic to different food types.

In this book I use different nuts for some of the dishes such as peanut butter and cashews etc.

There are also people with gluten allergies as well and many of these recipes contain gluten.

It is very important to always ask your guests or anyone you are preparing meals for if they have any food restrictions or allergies.

Also be wary of cross contamination with cooking utensils, cookware and equipment.

Always better to be safe!

Happy Cooking!

The Vegan Gorilla

Section 2

Conversion Table

VOLUME	IMPERIAL	METRIC
CONVERSION	1/4 tsp	1 ml
	1/2 tsp	2 ml
	3/4 tsp	4ml
	1 tsp	5ml
	1tbsp	15 ml
	2 tbsp	30 ml
	1/4 cup	60 ml
	1/2 cup	125 ml
	3/4 cup	175 ml
	1 cup	250 ml
OVEN TEMPERATURES	275 F	140 C
	300 F	150 C
	325 F	160C
	350 F	180C
	375 F	190C
	400 F	200C

Chapter 1

Where Do I Even Start?

OK so your in a bit of a pickle. (no vegan pun intended). You have a family member, friend or house guest coming over and they are vegan. WTF! What do I serve? I don't have time to make separate meals not to mention what to even make. Where do even I start?

Section 1

I Got Your Back

The reason I wanted to write about this is not to persuade you to be vegan. I wanted to help you figure out what to make for anyone you are entertaining that is vegan. If it sways you towards being Vegan even a few times a week that's great too.

Believe it or not we vegans eat more than lettuce. I've been vegan for 5 years now and lucky if I have 10 salads a year. (I really do have to start incorporating them more.)

In today's world being Vegan is becoming increasingly popular. Grocery stores are starting to stock shelves with vegan meats and cheese etc.

So I want to make this as simple as possible but without compromising flavors. You will see in some of my recipes where applicable you can purchase some of the ingredients at your local grocery store. If you don't have time to make the homemade recipe for example Vegan Burgers, Hummus etc. You can purchase them pre made at most grocery stores. Or you can make the recipes included for more fresh and flavorful meals.

I'm not a huge fan of pre made vegan products when its A) cheaper to make yourself and B) fresher and healthier. The point here is you have a few options and sometimes time is of the essence so convenience can help in a pinch.

I don't like to waste food whenever possible so you will notice throughout the book some of the recipes will tend to roll into each other. This makes it easier as well specially if your family member or guest will be staying for more than one meal.

For every recipe I will include a shopping list as a guide to confirm what you might already have in home or what you don't have and need to pick up at your local grocery store.

It is VERY IMPORTANT to always ask your guests if they have any food allergies before making and feeding them.

With vegan cooking we tend to use many nuts and seeds so keep in mind that cross contamination for anyone with allergies can be deadly.

If you're like me I tend to skip over all the reading in cook books and go straight to the recipes so I didn't want to keep adding in pages of fluff just for the purpose of having a higher page count to show value, etc.

So Let's Get Right Into It ....

Chapter 2

What Do I Need?

OK I'm cooking for a vegan. So what do I need?....Juicer? Lawnmower? Meditation? What?

Lettuce ....check

Carrots....check

Fruit....check

Meal Complete...check

Umm not just yet but nice try :)

Section 1

Basic Equipment

You will need some basic kitchen equipment for some of these recipes. Most people already have them and if not maybe you can borrow one if need be for the day.

Food Processor

Blender or Food Immersion Blender

Measuring Spoons

A good Chef Knife or Sharp Kitchen Knife

Pots and Frying Pans

Cutting Boards

Mixing Bowls

Grater: normally used for grating cheese

(Not the one for tractors) :)

Oven Pans for baking and pizza

Whisk and Utensils

Muffin Trays

Chapter 3

Breakfast of Champions

These Breakfasts are super easy to make and 100 percent vegan. Nothing fancy just a few spins on the foods most people eat already.

Note:

Herbs & Spices are big in Vegan cooking and make such an impact on flavor.

Section 1

Tofu Scramble & Hash Browns

This Is A Great Breakfast With A Lot Of Protein From The Tofu. Add Side Of Toast & 0 J

Ingredients

1/2 block of extra firm tofu (choose organic)

1/2 red pepper

1/2 scallion or (onion)

1 potato cubed or shredded

1 tablespoon olive oil

2 slices of bread of choice

2 tablespoons of peanut butter

Spices

1 teaspoon turmeric

1 teaspoon parsley

1 tablespoon of black salt

1 teaspoon of cracked black pepper

1 clove of garlic

Section 2

Putting It All Together

This is one of my favorites for breakfast and so easy to put together. If your guests or family members don't like peppers or onions you can definitely swap them out for something else. Throw in asparagus or broccoli instead or spice it up with some hot sauce even. The combinations are only limited to your taste buds. So feel free to be creative here.

Steps

I) Slice the red pepper into small cubes. Try to keep the cube sizes similar so they cook evenly.

2) Peel the potato first. Then using a cheese grater shred the raw potato.

3) Chop the shallot into small even cubes. With a medium to low heat add the olive oil and the shallots. Give them a little stir and let them cook until translucent.

4) Add the chopped garlic, red pepper and shredded potato. Stir the ingredients together and allow them to sauté for a few minutes.

5) Add the salt and cracked pepper and cook on medium high giving it a few stirs so everything cooks evenly.

6) Now take the tofu block and press it on a paper towel to get any leftover moisture out of it. Then in a separate bowl crumble the tofu up with your fingers mimicking a scrambled egg look.

7) Add the turmeric and parsley and give it a mix. You will notice the tofu will take on the color of the turmeric and will look like eggs.

8) Once it is mixed well add the tofu to the pan with the rest of the ingredients already cooking.

9) Continue to cook for a few minutes on medium high. Stir and flip to ensure everything is cooked evenly. Tofu doesn't take long to cook as your merely heating up and blending it with the rest of the ingredients.

10) Meanwhile pop a few slices of bread in the toaster then butter with peanut butter and pour a glass of orange juice.

Done

Simple, filling and delicious.

This makes enough for one large serving.

Gorilla Note*: Black salt you can find in a health food store. It makes a world of difference and gives it the egg taste. If you can't find any you can use regular sea salt.*

Nice Work And You Don't Have To Be Vegan To Eat It

Sometimes it's just that simple

Ingredients to Buy

Ingredients	Have It	Buy It
Extra Firm Tofu	☆	☐
Red Pepper	☆	☐
Scallion or onion	☆	☐
Potato	☆	☐
Olive Oil	☆	☐
Bread of choice	☆	☐
Peanut Butter	☆	☐
Turmeric Parsley	☆	☐
Black Salt	☆	☐
Cracked Black Pepper	☆	☐
Clove of garlic	☆	☐
	☆	☐
	☆	☐
	☆	☐
	☆	☐

Section 3

Peanut Butter & Banana Pancakes

Makes About 8 - 10 Pancakes

Peanut Butter Pancakes

Dry Ingredients

1 cup of white flour

1 teaspoon baking powder

1 tablespoon of brown sugar

1 pinch of salt

1/2 of 1 banana

Wet Ingredients

1 1/4 cup of soy or almond milk (non dairy)

2 tablespoons of peanut butter

1 tablespoon of banana extract

1 tablespoon of lemon juice

4 tablespoons of maple syrup

Step 1

Mix all the dry ingredients in a bowl except for the banana. Set that aside. I find using a whisk works best to get the ingredients blended well.

Step 2

In a separate bowl add all the wet ingredients together and mix well. ***Except The Peanut Butter & Maple Syrup.***

Step 3

Now mix the wet ingredients into the bowl with the dry ingredients. Do not over mix. You want to create a thick batter consistency that will run off your spoon slowly. A few lumps in the batter is fine. Let the batter rest for a few min.

Step 4

Heat up your frying pan or skillet with a table spoon of olive oil or non stick spray oil. I like to put my pan on a medium high.

Step 5

Using a large spoon add the batter to the frying pan. Continue to add more batter to the middle of the pancake until you reach your desired size you want. 4-5 inches is good.

Its Coming Together

Vegan Pancakes ..... Not When I was a Kid

Section 4

I Can See The Finish Line

Step 6

Allow the pancakes to cook for a minute or 2. You will see bubbles starting to form in the batter. Check the underside of the pancake and when its golden brown flip them over to cook the other side.

Step 7

In a small pot add the peanut butter and maple syrup. On medium low heat stir until melted and mixed together.

Next Stack pancakes on top of each other and add a little vegan butter if desired. Now take your banana and chop it up in 1/2 inch widths and place on top of the pancakes.

Step 8

Drizzle over the top of the pancakes the peanut butter maple syrup sauce. Add a side of coffee or tea and enjoy.

Repeat and Eat Again

Ingredients To Buy

Ingredients	Have It	Buy It
White Flour	☆	☐
Baking Powder	☆	☐
Brown Sugar	☆	☐
Salt	☆	☐
Banana	☆	☐
Almond Milk	☆	☐
Peanut Butter	☆	☐
Banana Extract	☆	☐
Lemon Juice	☆	☐
Maple Syrup	☆	☐
	☆	☐
	☆	☐
	☆	☐
	☆	☐
	☆	☐

Section 5

ALT Sandwich

Avocado, Lettuce & Tomato Sandwich

Ingredients

1 ripe avocado

1 ripe tomato

A few leaves of fresh crisp iceberg lettuce

2 slices of bread (your choice)

4 tablespoons of hummus

(sauces & dip section)

salt & pepper to taste

Section 6

ALT Making It Happen

Step 1

Slice open the avocado and cut into strips.

If you never had to opened an avocado then follow these easy steps. **I)** Cut the avocado all around starting from the top and go right down to the bottom and back up to the top again. You can only go so deep because of the pitt inside. **2)** Twist the 2 halves apart. **3)** Using your knife in a light chop motion hit the centre of the pitt with the knife blade, 3) Hold the half avocado firmly in one hand and twist the knife with the other and the pitt will release. **4)** Using your knife cut the outline of the skin on the inside following the shape of the avocado. s) Now cut in strips and remove from the skin. Well Done!

Step 2

Slice the tomato evenly apart as best as you can.

Step 3

Toast your bread until a crispy golden brown.

Step 4

Add the hummus to the toast on both slices and layer on avocado, tomato and lettuce. Salt and pepper to taste. **Done!**

Ingredients To Buy

Ingredients	Have It	Buy It
Avocado	★	☐
Tomato	★	☐
Iceberg Lettuce	★	☐
Hummus (In sauce and dip section)	★	☐
Salt	★	☐
Pepper	★	☐
	★	☐
	★	☐
	★	☐
	★	☐
	★	☐
	★	☐
	★	☐
	★	☐

Section 7

Oatmeal 101

Single Serving

Ingredients

1/2 cup of rolled oats

3/4 cups of water

1/2 cup of fruit of your choice

1 teaspoon of cinnamon

Step 1

Combine the oats and water in a sauce pan on medium high.

Bring to a boil and reduce heat to medium.

Step 2

Allow oatmeal to continue to cook stirring often until the oatmeal starts to thicken up.

Gorilla Note: *If you want a more runny oatmeal just add a bit more water until thickness is desired.*

Step 3

Plate oatmeal adding the teaspoon of cinnamon over top and fresh fruit of your choice.

You can also add a drizzle of Maple syrup if desired.

This is Super easy to make and so good for you!

You can be creative

Choose whatever fruit you have and chop up and add.

Ingredients To Buy

Ingredients	Have It	Buy It
Rolled Oats	★	☐
Fruit of your choice	★	☐
Cinnamon	★	☐
Water	★	☐
	★	☐
	★	☐
	★	☐
	★	☐
	★	☐
	★	☐
	★	☐
	★	☐
	★	☐
	★	☐

Section 8

Simple Sexy Smoothie Wait! What?

Delicious Breakfast Smoothie With Protein To Start Your Day

Ingredients

1 cup of dairy free milk of choice

1 cup of frozen fruit mix berries

1/2 an avocado

2 tablespoons of peanut butter

Step 1

Add all the ingredients into a blender

Note: *If you don't have frozen fruit add the fruit you have with a few ice cubes.*

Step 2

Pulse several times to break up the ingredients.

Step 3

Blend until smooth

(Add more milk if you desire a thinner smoothie)

Ingredients To Buy

Ingredients	Have It	Buy It
Dairy free milk of your choice	★	☐
Frozen fruit mixed berries	★	☐
Avocado	★	☐
Peanut Butter	★	☐
	★	☐
	★	☐
	★	☐
	★	☐
	★	☐
	★	☐
	★	☐
	★	☐
	★	☐
	★	☐

Chapter 4

Lunch & Munch

Here are some delicious lunch ideas to make. Add some sides like fresh veggies and salads or be naughty and add fries. You can combine a few of them together for a larger meal if you want too.

Section 1

Tofu Kabobs

Summer Time You Can BBQ These For A More Smokey Flavor

Ingredients

1/2 block of extra firm tofu

1 potato

6 button mushrooms

1/2 Spanish red or yellow onion

2 cups of spinach

Marinade Ingredients

1/2 cup soy sauce

1 garlic clove chopped fine

2 tablespoons of lemon juice

1/2 teaspoon of salt

1/2 teaspoon of cracked pepper

Extra

2 kabobs sticks soaked in cold water

Section 2

Kaboom!

Pre heat the oven to 350 deg F

Step 1

In a separate bowl combine the ingredients of the marinade sauce. Give it a good stir and set to the side.

Step 2

Using the button mushrooms as a size indicator. Take the tofu and cut into even cubes. Now slice the onions, potato and mushrooms in similar size. This will help with cooking it all evenly.

Step 3

Place the tofu cubes and add it to the marinade bowl making sure they all get covered evenly. Let it continue to sit in the marinade while you cut and wash the rest of the vegetables.

Gorilla Note:

Boil the potatoes first for a bit to pre cook them. They will take longer than the rest to cook. Be careful when handling the potatoes they may break away from the skewers if you're not gentle.

Section 3
Plate These On A Bed Of Spinach And Drizzle Gorilla Mayo Sauce (see sauces)

Assembling the Kabob

Step 4

Take I of the kabob sticks and spear it through the middle of a tofu piece.

Next do the same thing to the potato, mushrooms and onions.

Repeat the same thing 2 or 3 more times: Cap the bottom off with tofu.

There should be tofu at the top and bottom and 2 in between the kabob stick.

Step 5

Now repeat process to the second kabob stick.

Step 6

If its summer time or you have access to a year round bbq then of course put these babies on the grill. If not then using the oven bake on an oven rack for 30 min at 350 deg F.

Makes for Large Single Serving Size

Ingredients To Buy

Ingredients	Have It	Buy It
Extra firm tofu		
Potato		
Button Mushrooms		
Spanish or yellow onions		
Spinach		
Soy sauce Garlic clove		
Lemon juice		
Salt		
Cracked pepper		
Kabobs sticks		

Section 4

Warm Broccoli & Tofu Wrap

One Of My Favorites Wraps To Make

Ingredients

4 tablespoons of hummus & a little extra for dipping

1/2 avocado

handful of alfalfa sprouts or greens

5 pieces of broccoli

1 clove of garlic finely chopped

2 tablespoons of olive oil

2 large pieces of baked tofu (*see next recipe*)

1 - 10 inch tortilla wrap

salt & pepper to taste

Section 5

Wrap Not Rap :) But That's Good Too!

Step 1

In a small frying pan on medium high add the olive oil, broccoli and a dash of salt. Continue to cook until broccoli is tender to the penetration of a fork.

Step 2

Continue to cook adding in the chopped garlic and sauté it with the broccoli. Watch closely as garlic will burn quickly and leave a pungent taste if over cooked.

Step 3

The baked tofu you can have cold or you can heat it up in the oven for a few minutes.

Step 4

Lay the tortilla flat down. Spread the hummus on the wrap.

In the middle of the wrap add the tofu, broccoli, avocado and alfalfa sprouts forming a straight line across the middle of the tortilla. Then season with salt and pepper.

Section 6

Done! That's A Wrap!

Step 5

From the bottom pull the wrap up past the assembled ingredients just past the line formation.

Tuck the little bit of excess wrap under the ingredients pulling it slightly back towards you and forming a roll.

Now continue to roll the tortilla towards the top until about 3/ 4 of the way up. Fold the ends in tucking them under the roll and continue to roll to the end.

Step 6

Cut the wrap on a diagonal and add a side of potato chips and you have one happy vegan.

Gorilla Note:

This is enough for I wrap. If you want to make 2 just double the recipe.

Ingredients To Buy

Ingredients	Have It	Buy It
Hummus		
Avocado		
Alfalfa sprouts		
Greens		
Broccoli		
Clove of garlic		
Olive oil		
Baked tofu (See next recipe)		
Tortilla wrap		
Salt		
Pepper		

Section 7

Baked Tofu

This Is More Than A Serving But Save Some And You Can Use For The Wrap

Ingredients

1 block of extra firm tofu

1/4 cup of soy sauce or tamari sauce

1 garlic clove finely chopped

1 tablespoon of onion powder 1r tablespoon of liquid smoke (*optional*)

1 tablespoon of hot sauce (*your choice*)

parchment paper

cooking spray or tablespoon of olive oil

Section 8

Many Combinations To Use In Other Recipes

Step 1

Pre heat oven to 350 deg

Step 2

Cut the tofu in blocks approximately 1 1/2 inch thick.

Step 3

Add the remaining ingredients in a casserole bowl and mix together.

Place the strips of tofu in the marinade flipping them over to make sure they are fully covered in marinade.

Allow to sit for 15 minutes.

Step 4

On a sheet pan place the parchment paper and lightly spray with oil or brush the olive oil on.

Lay the tofu down and bake for approximately 15 minutes. Flip and cook for another 10-12 minutes.

Let cool slightly then serve with a side of veggies or on top of a salad.

Ingredients To Buy

Ingredients	Have It	Buy It
Block of extra firm tofu		
Soy sauce of tamari sauce		
Garlic clove		
Onion powder		
Liquid smoke (Optional)		
Hot sauce (Your choice)		
Parchment paper		
Cooking spray or olive oil		

Section 9

Gorilla Poutine

Here You Can Make Your Own Fries Or Use The Store Bought Ones.

Fries Ingredients

potatoes

olive oil

oregano

parsley

salt

Gravy Ingredients

2 cups of sliced mushrooms

1 1/2 cups of vegetable broth

1/4 cup diced onions & 2 tablespoons of olive oil

2 tablespoons of soy sauce or tamari

1 clove garlic finely chopped

1 tablespoon of onion salt

2 tablespoons of corn starch or flour

Section 10

This Poutine is no Routine :)

Gorilla Feta Ingredients

Half block of extra firm tofu

1/4 cup of Gorilla Zesty Dip sauce

(see sauce section just leave out the sriracha)

2 tablespoons of red wine vinegar

1 tablespoon of oregano and parsley

salt and pepper to taste

Step 1

Pre heat oven to 350 degrees F

In a bowl mix the Gorilla Mayo sauce, red wine vinegar, oregano and salt and pepper. Give it a few stirs then using your fingers crumble the tofu in the sauce covering all parts of the tofu.

Set aside and let it marinate while you prepare the rest of the recipe.

Step 2

Slice the potatoes in strips and mix in the olive oil, oregano, salt and parsley.

Place on baking sheet and cook for approximately 30-45 minutes or until golden brown.

Note: *You can also use store bought bag fries if you wish*

Step 3

In a sauce pan add the olive oil and onions and cook on medium high for a few minutes until the onions turn translucent.

Then add in the garlic and mushrooms and continue cooking until the mushrooms are fully cooked.

Next add in the vegetable broth, soy sauce or tamari and onion salt and bring to a light boil for a few minutes.

Next reduce the heat to a simmer. Now add in the corn starch or white flour and create a slurry while continuing to stir.

Allow the gravy to slowly thicken while occasionally stirring. If you want your gravy a little thicker you can add more corn starch. If you want it a little thinner you can add more vegetable broth.

Section 11

Poutining It All Together Now :)

Assembling the Poutine

Final Step

The fun part now.

In either a bowl or plate add the potato fries.

Cover them with the mushroom gravy then take some of the Gorilla Feta crumble and place it on top of the gravy. Add some salt and cracked pepper to taste and enjoy!

You can enjoy it on its own. It's filling or you can combine it with any of the other recipes.

Ingredients To Buy

Ingredients	Have It	Buy It
Potatoes	☆	☐
Olive oil	☆	☐
Oregano	☆	☐
Parsley	☆	☐
Salt	☆	☐
Mushrooms	☆	☐
Vegetable broth	☆	☐
Onions	☆	☐
Olive oil	☆	☐
Soy sauce or tamari	☆	☐
Clove garlic	☆	☐
Onion salt	☆	☐
Corn starch or flour	☆	☐
	☆	☐
	☆	☐

Section 12

Cauliflower Mushroom Soup

Many Ingredients But Worth It In The End.

Ingredients

4 cups of chopped cauliflower

2 cups of sliced mushrooms

4 cups of vegetable broth

2 cups of water

1 can of organic coconut cream

1 shallot onion

2 tablespoons of salt

2 tablespoons of cracked pepper

1 tablespoon of basil

1 tablespoon of onion powder

1 tablespoon of chipotle powder

1 tablespoon of coriander

1 tablespoon of oregano

1 tablespoon of liquid amino or soy sauce

4 tablespoons of nutritional yeast

Section 13

"No Soup For You" - Seinfeld But This One You Can :)

Step 1

In a large pot add the olive oil and onions and cook on medium high for a few minutes until the onions turn translucent.

Then add in the salt, pepper, garlic and mushrooms and continue cooking until the mushrooms are fully cooked. Scoop out most of the mushrooms only and set aside.

Step 2

Leaving it on medium high add the broth and water and 2 cups of cauliflower. Next the can of coconut cream and the remaining ingredients Except for 2 cups of cauliflower and the mushrooms.

Step 3

Bring to a boil while stirring occasionally for 10 - 15 minutes. By this time the cauliflower should be soft.

Now Reduce the heat to a simmer.

Using an immersion blender carefully place the blade below the liquid line before you turn it on. This should prevent any splash up. ***BE EXTREMELTCAREFUL*** as this could splash on you and burn.

Section 14

Almost Done. NEXT!!!

Step 3 continued ...

Continue to blend until the soup and cauliflower has completely liquefied.

Gorilla Note: If you do not have an immersion blender you can transfer the soup into a regular blender and purify for a few minutes and transfer back to the pot. Again being careful not to burn yourself with the hot soup.

Step 4

Now add in the remainder 2 cups of finely chopped cauliflower and the mushrooms that you set aside earlier.

Keep soup on a low simmer for another 15-20 minutes.

Step 5

If you want to add some extra flavor and you have some toasted sesame oil on hand then add a few drops on top of the soup with some cilantro before serving. Add a side of crusty toast.

Delish!!

Ingredients To Buy

Ingredients	Have it	Buy It
Cauliflower	★	☐
Mushrooms	★	☐
Vegetable broth	★	☐
Can of organic coconut cream	★	☐
Shallot or onion	★	☐
Salt	★	☐
Cracked pepper	★	☐
Basil	★	☐
Onion powder	★	☐
Chipotle powder	★	☐
Coriander	★	☐
Oregano	★	☐
Liquid amino or soy sauce	★	☐
Nutritional yeast	★	☐
	★	☐

Chapter 5

Fast & Easy Dinners

No need to be overwhelmed here. These are simple but delicious meals that will not only satisfy your guests and or yourself but leaving them wanting more.

Section 1

Cauliflower Steak .. Healthy and Filling

This Makes Dinner For Two Or For One Very Hungry Vegan :)

Ingredients

1 medium sized cauliflower

1 1/2 cups of vegetable broth

1 cup of water

3 garlic cloves finely chopped

1 teaspoon of salt

1 teaspoon of pepper

1 bay leave

1 tablespoon of non dairy butter

Mushroom Gravy

See sauces

Section 2

No Animals Were Harmed In This Meal

Step 1

Preheat oven to 350 degrees F

Cut the cauliflower in half Keeping the core stem intact as this will hold it together.

Cut the pieces at least 1 1/2 inches thick. Then place in a deep baking pan.

Step 2

Mix the rest of the ingredients together ***Except*** the non dairy butter and pour over top of the cauliflower. Cover the dish with foil completely and bake in the oven for approximately 40-45 minutes on the medium rack in the oven.

Gorilla Note: The cauliflower should be cooked through but still a bit firm.

Step 3

Carefully remove the cauliflower from the oven and dish. Note there will be very hot steam from the foil once it is removed so be cautious. Place the cauliflower on a paper towel and blot both sides dry.

Section 3

Steak Your Claim or Claim Your Steak!

Step 4

Heat a large frying pan up over medium to high heat (even better if you have cast iron).Once hot add the non dairy butter and let the cauliflower cook for a few minutes until golden brown then flip and repeat on the other side.

Step 5

To finish make the mushroom gravy from the sauce section of this book and generously cover the cauliflower with it.

This is a great meal in itself The large portion of cauliflower ends with a sear from the pan and covered with a mushroom gravy. This will satisfy your pickiest vegan guests out there.

Enjoy!

Ingredients To Buy

Ingredients	Have It	Buy It
Medium sized cauliflower	☆	☐
Vegetable broth	☆	☐
Water	☆	☐
Garlic cloves	☆	☐
Salt	☆	☐
Cracked pepper	☆	☐
Bay leaf	☆	☐
Non dairy butter	☆	☐
Mushroom gravy see sauces	☆	☐
	☆	☐
	☆	☐
	☆	☐
	☆	☐
	☆	☐
	☆	☐

Section 4

Pizza Gorilla Style

No, I Didn't Forget The Sauce Lol.

Pizza Dough Ingredients

2 cups of all purpose flour + extra for kneading

3/4 cup luke warm water

1 teaspoon of active dry yeast

1 1/2 teaspoons of salt

1 tablespoon of olive oil

Pizza Topping Ingredients

1 cup kalamata olives

1 cup of sliced onions

2 cups of sliced mushrooms

1 tablespoon of oregano

1 tablespoon of garlic powder

4 tablespoons of olive oil for brushing

Handful of fresh basil

Section 5

Gorilla Style Pizza

Step 1

Gorilla Note: If you don't have time to make your own dough you can certainly buy it pre made at most grocery stores.

Pour the luke warm water and yeast into a bowl and let sit until the yeast has dissolved.

Next add the salt and flour a little at a time while mixing with your hands to form a dough. *You can use a stand alone mixer if you have one with a kneading hook. Continue to add the flour until it is all in and formed into a dough ball.*

Step 2

Now using a little extra flour on the counter start kneading the dough. This activates the gluten in the flour. Do this for approximately 7 - 10 minutes. Add more flour if the dough starts to stick to your hands during this process.

If you're unsure how to knead dough there are many simple techniques you can you tube for a demonstration.

Step 3

Using the olive oil put a light film of oil on the dough and leave it in the bowl. Cover firmly with plastic wrap and let sit to rise.

Section 6

Pizza Without Sauce & Cheese Oh My!

Step 4 Pre Heat Oven to 375 Degrees F

After 1 - 1.5 hours the dough is ready to be shaped.

You can use a rolling pin to spread the dough out but I find using my hands works very well. Sprinkle your pan with a little more flour and press out the dough to your desired size and crust thickness. *I made mine into approximately a r6 inch round.*

Step 5 Adding The Toppings

Now take some of the olive oil and brush it all over the top of the dough. Next sprinkle the garlic salt and oregano.

Now distribute in an even manner the olives, onions and mushrooms. Add a little salt and cracked peeper if you like as well.

Next drizzle the remainder of the olive oil over the ingredients.

Bake for approximately 30 minutes until crust is cooked throughout.

Done.

Gorilla Note: *You will not miss the cheese nor the sauce with this one as the olive oil keeps it moist and the flavor combinations is very tasty. The olives add a nice salty flavor for balance.*

Ingredients To Buy

Ingredients	Have It	Buy It
All purpose flour	★	☐
Active dry yeast	★	☐
Salt	★	☐
Olive oil	★	☐
Kalamata olives	★	☐
Sliced mushrooms	★	☐
Oregano	★	☐
Garlic powder	★	☐
Olive oil	★	☐
Fresh basil	★	☐
	★	☐
	★	☐
	★	☐
	★	☐
	★	☐

Section 7

Pasta With Avocado Pesto

You're Going To Make This One More Than Once :)

Ingredients

1 package of penne pasta

2 cups of tightly packed basil

2 finely chopped garlic cloves

3 heaping tablespoons of nutritional yeast

1 tablespoon of sea salt

1 avocado

1/4 cup of vegetable stock

2 tablespoons of olive oil

Section 8

Mama Mia

Step 1

Start with the boiling some water for the pasta. ***DO NOT*** add oil to the water as this will coat the pasta and the sauce will not stick as well to the penne. Do add enough salt though so that the water has a bit of a salty taste to it.

Once it starts to boil add in your pasta and let cook to the desired tenderness you prefer.

(Some like it al dente others do not)

Step 2

Add the remaining ingredients to your food processor and pulse it until it is mostly chopped.

Step 3

Now turn the processor on low and mix until smooth and creamy.

Step 4

Once the pasta is cooked drain the water well and stir in the pesto sauce. Mix well and serve.

It's That Simple!

Ingredients To Buy

Ingredients	Have It	Buy It
Penne pasta	☆	☐
Basil	☆	☐
Garlic clove	☆	☐
Nutritional yeast	☆	☐
Sea salt	☆	☐
Avocado	☆	☐
Vegetable stock	☆	☐
Olive oil	☆	☐
	☆	☐
	☆	☐
	☆	☐
	☆	☐
	☆	☐
	☆	☐
	☆	☐

Section 9

Portobello And Mashed Dill Potatoes

These Meaty Mushrooms Will Make Your Day.

Ingredients

2 large Portobello mushrooms

2 large peeled potatoes

1 cup of vegetable broth

1/4 cup of tamari or soy sauce

2 cloves of garlic chopped finely

1/2 tablespoon of sea salt

1/2 tablespoon of cracked pepper

1/3 cup of chopped fresh dill

2 tablespoons of fresh lemon juice

1 teaspoon of thyme

1/2 cup of water

2 tablespoons of non dairy butter

1/4 cup of non dairy milk

Section 10

No Time To Dilly Dally

Step 1

In a deep dish add and whisk together the:

1 cup of vegetable broth

1/4 cup of tamari or soy sauce

2 cloves of garlic chopped finely

1 tablespoon of sea salt

1 tablespoon of pepper

2 tablespoons of lemon juice

1 teaspoon of thyme

1/2 cup of water

Step 2 Preheat Oven to 350 degrees F

Clean & place both Portobello mushrooms gill side up in the oven dish and pour the marinade over both mushrooms generously. Cover the dish with foil and place in oven on medium rack for 15 minutes.

Section 11

Serve Potatoes On Top & Underneath

Step 3 ***while the mushrooms are cooking***

Boil the potatoes on medium high until a fork and easily penetrate into the centre. Approximately 20-25 minutes. *After IS minutes remove the foil from the dish in the oven and continue to bake for another 10 minutes.*

Step 4

Drain the water from the potatoes then start to mash them up in a pot. Do this on the same burner you just turned off to keep things warm.

Step 5

Add:

2 tablespoons of non dairy butter

1 4 cup of non dairy milk a little at a time

1/4 cup of chopped dill

Using a potato masher or fork continue to smash and mix the potatoes until soft and creamy. You should be able to run a fork through the potatoes separating them. If too runny then let it sit a few minutes longer until thickened.

Ingredients To Buy

Ingredients	Have It	Buy It
Large Portobello mushrooms	☆	☐
Potatoes	☆	☐
Vegetable broth	☆	☐
Tamari or soy sauce	☆	☐
Clove of garlic	☆	☐
Sea salt	☆	☐
Cracked pepper	☆	☐
Fresh dill	☆	☐
Fresh lemon juice	☆	☐
Thyme	☆	☐
Water	☆	☐
Non dairy butter	☆	☐
Non dairy milk	☆	☐
	☆	☐
	☆	☐

Section 12

Mmm Mushroom & Lentil Bean

This Burger Has Great Texture And Substance

Ingredients

1/2 cup ***cooked*** bulgur grain

1 cup canned lentil beans, mashed

1 tablespoon olive oil & (*extra for frying*)

3-4-medium mushrooms chopped

1/2 stalk celery finely chopped

1/2 small carrot finely chopped

1/4 red onion finely chopped

2 cloves garlic finely minced

1 teaspoon salt

1 cup bread crumbs

1 tablespoon ground chia seeds

2 tablespoons soy sauce

1 tablespoon of ground fennel seeds

2 tablespoons of bbq sauce

1 tablespoon of lemon juice

Section 13

The Burger Process :)

Step 1

In a large pan on medium high heat, add the chopped celery, carrot, onion, mushrooms, garlic and salt. *(make sure these veggies are finely chopped and diced first).* Cook until tender.

Step 2

Now add the precooked bulgur grain, smashed lentils, bread crumbs, ground chia seeds, soy sauce, bbq sauce, lemon and ground fennel seeds. Now stir until the mixture gets very thick and hard to stir.

Step 3

Place mixture in the fridge and let rest for about an hour. This will help thicken it up even more.

Step 4

After the mixture has set take out of the fridge and start to form the patties with your hands. First into a ball then pressing down to the desired thickness you want.

Heat a frying pan up with a little oil on medium high heat and cook the burgers approximately 3-5 min each side.

Section 14

Almost There

Step 5

Fry burgers with a little oil in your favorite frying pan. Even better if you have cast iron.

Now you can assemble the burgers. You can toast the buns or warm them up and the choice of condiments are unlimited to your taste buds.

I like to use a little Gorilla Mayo on mine with avocado slices, onions, pickles and lettuce.

Serve with a small side salad or home fries.

Cheers!

Gorilla Note: This will make a few burgers pending how big you make them. They freeze well too! You can use another grain if you don't have bulgur grain.

Gorilla Note 2: I used a hamburger mould ($2.99) to get perfect circles and press them but you can use your hands just as easy.

Ingredients To Buy

Ingredients	Have It	Buy It
Cooked bulgar grain	☆	☐
Lentil beans	☆	☐
Olive oil / Salt	☆	☐
Medium mushrooms	☆	☐
Celery	☆	☐
Small carrot	☆	☐
Red onion	☆	☐
Garlic cloves	☆	☐
Bread crumbs	☆	☐
Ground chia seeds	☆	☐
Soy sauce	☆	☐
Fennel seeds	☆	☐
bbq sauce	☆	☐
lemon juice	☆	☐
	☆	☐

Chapter 6

Desserts Vegan Style

These desserts are simple to make for the most part. There are so many good variations you can spin on these so feel free to be creative with them if you want to put your own stamp on it. :)

Section 1

Banana Sweet Special

This Is Super Easy. Only 3 Ingredients

Ingredients

1 large banana

1 teaspoon of cinnamon

3 tablespoons of maple syrup

Section 2

Easy Peasy

Step 1

Slice bananas to about r/ 4 inch thickness

Step2

Layer the banana on a plate and cover with the maple syrup

Step 3

Sprinkle on the cinnamon

It's simple yet delicious

Enjoy!

Ingredients To Buy

Ingredients	Have It	Buy It
Large banana	★	☐
Cinnamon	★	☐
Maple syrup	★	☐
	★	☐
	★	☐
	★	☐
	★	☐
	★	☐
	★	☐
	★	☐
	★	☐
	★	☐
	★	☐
	★	☐

Section 3

Fruit Kabob With Chocolate Sauce

You Might Want To Make A Few Of These :)

Ingredients

A few long kabob skewers

1 banana sliced in 1/2 inch thickness apart 6 straw-berries

1 kiwi

4 oz of dark chocolate without milk in it

(I use 72% cocoa dark chocolate)

1/2 cup of non dairy milk

1/2 teaspoon of sea salt

1 teaspoon of olive oil

Section 4

Saucy Goodness Continued

Step 1

Skewer the bananas, kiwis, strawberries and grapes in a rhythmic order on each skewer and set aside on plate.

Step 2

Finely chop all the dark chocolate and place into a heatproof bowl. (stainless steel works well).

Step 3

On medium high heat add the non dairy milk and salt and bring to a low boil. Be careful not to overcook and burn.

Once boiled remove and pour the non dairy milk over the dark chocolate and cover immediately with a plate. Give it a couple swirls to make sure the milk covers the chocolate completely. Let sit for 4-5 minutes.

Step 4

Remove plate and begin to whisk the chocolate until smooth and glossy. (Do not over mix). Now add the olive oil and whisk again.

Step 5 *Place in dipping bowl and allow to thicken at room temperature*

Ingredients To Buy

Ingredients	Have It	Buy It
Kabob skewers		
Banana		
Strawberries		
Kiwi		
Dark chocolate without milk		
I use 72% cocoa dark chocolate		
Non dairy milk		
Sea salt		
Olive oil		

Section 5

Cake In A Cup ... What ??

The Gorilla Chocolate Cup Cake ... Not To Be Confused With Cupcake .. :)

Ingredients

4 generous tablespoons of white flour

3 1/2 teaspoons cocoa

1 pinch of salt

2 tablespoons of maple syrup

1/2 teaspoon of baking powder

1 teaspoon of vanilla extract

1/2 cup + 2 tablespoons of soy milk

1/4 cup dark chocolate grated or chopped

Section 6

Too Good Not To Make Yourself One :)

Step 1

Place to the side the shredded dark chocolate for now.

Place all the dry ingredients in a small mixing bowl and give it a few whisks to mix it together well.

Then in a separate bowl or cup mix the wet ingredients together giving it a good stir.

Step 2

Pour the wet ingredients in with the dry and mix well until you have a cake batter mixture.

Step 3

Pour half the batter into a coffee mug. Add half the shredded dark chocolate in and fill the remainder of the batter into the cup. Now sprinkle the remaining dark chocolate evenly on top.

Step 4

Place in the microwave for approximately 2 minutes. Check for doneness. *Pending on your microwave you might need+ or - more seconds.*

Done!

Ingredients To Buy

Ingredients	Have It	Buy It
White flour	★	☐
Cocoa	★	☐
Salt	★	☐
Maple syrup	★	☐
Baking powder	★	☐
Vanilla extract	★	☐
Soy milk	★	☐
Dark chocolate	★	☐
	★	☐
	★	☐
	★	☐
	★	☐
	★	☐
	★	☐
	★	☐

Section 7

Chia Pudding

This One You Need To Plan A Day Ahead

Ingredients

1 cup of non dairy milk

2 tablespoons chia seeds

1 teaspoon vanilla extract

1 tablespoon of maple syrup

fresh fruit for topping

a few chopped walnuts

1 teaspoon of cocoa

Section 8

CH .. CH .. CH .. Chia!

Step 1

In a mason jar or container with a lid add all the ingredients.

Step 2

Mix very well to prevent the chia seeds from clumping together. Place into the refrigerator.

Step 3

Put a lid on or cover and every 30 minutes or so give it a good shake. You only have to do this a few times as the chia seeds will start to absorb the milk and flavors and begin to expand.

Step 4

Refrigerate for a few hours but best to leave it over night to really thicken.

Step 5

When ready to serve top with fresh fruit of choice and a few chopped walnuts.

Gorilla Note: Very Filling and a good breakfast alternative as well.

Ingredients To Buy

Ingredients	Have It	Buy It
Non dairy milk	★	☐
Chia seeds 1	★	☐
Vanilla extract	★	☐
Maple syrup	★	☐
Fresh fruit	★	☐
Walnuts	★	☐
Cocoa	★	☐
	★	☐
	★	☐
	★	☐
	★	☐
	★	☐
	★	☐
	★	☐
	★	☐

Section 9

Chocolate Oatmeal Fudge

Very Rich In Flavor

Ingredients

1 1/4 cups of almond milk

5 medjool dates pitted

1/2 teaspoon of salt

2 tablespoons of cocoa

4 tablespoons of dried cranberries or raisons + a few extra for topping when plating

3/4 cup of dry oats

Section 10

Warm Chocolate Sweetness

Step 1

Add the dates, milk, salt and cocoa to your blender and blend until smooth.

Step 2

Pour the wet mixture in a sauce pan add the oats and cranberries. Allow to simmer (low heat a few bubbles but not boiling) for approximately 6-9 minutes.

Step 3

Once finished simmering scoop the mixture into small serving dishes. Sprinkle with a pinch of sea salt and a few more cranberries and serve.

Gorilla Note: Double up the recipe and make one for yourself You won't regret it.

Ingredients To Buy

Ingredients	Have It	Buy It
Almond Milk	★	☐
Medjool dates	★	☐
Salt	★	☐
Cocoa	★	☐
Dried cranberries or raisons	★	☐
	★	☐
	★	☐
	★	☐
	★	☐
	★	☐
	★	☐
	★	☐
	★	☐
	★	☐

Chapter 7

Let's Get Saucy

These staple sauces I wanted to include because they have many uses that can be enjoyed in multiple recipes vegan or not. Master these and they will be your go to for many occasions.

Section 1

Holy Moly Guacamole

You're Going To Love This One

Ingredients

3 avocados

1 garlic clove

half of a small jalapeno pepper

half of one tomato

1/2 of one shallot onion

1/4 cup of chopped cilantro

1/2 of one lime

1 1/2 tablespoons of sea salt

Section 2

Guacamole Glam Serve with pita bread or nacho chips

Step 1

Cut and remove the pit and skin of the 3 avocados.

Spoon out the inside of the tomato half removing the seeds.

Remove the seeds from the half jalapeno pepper.

Step 2

Dice the shallot, jalapeno, garlic clove and tomato in small pieces.

Try about 1/4 inch x 1/4 inch in size for each.

Step 3

In a mixing bowl add all the chopped ingredients at this point.

Using a fork start to press and mix the avocado and ingredients together.

Now add the juice of half a lime and the sea salt and continue to mash and mix. Do not puree just make it a little chunky.

Step 4

Chop the cilantro into small pieces. (you can bunch together to cut) then add to the guacamole and give it a few final stirs.

Ingredients To Buy

Ingredients	Have It	Buy It
Avocados	★	☐
Jalapeno pepper	★	☐
Tomato shallot onion	★	☐
Lime	★	☐
Sea salt	★	☐
	★	☐
	★	☐
	★	☐
	★	☐
	★	☐
	★	☐
	★	☐
	★	☐
	★	☐

Section 3

Chocolate Gorilla Sauce

This Has So Many Uses You Can Apply Too.

Ingredients

4 oz of dark chocolate without milk in it

(I use 72% cocoa dark chocolate)

1/2 cup of non dairy milk

1/2 teaspoon of sea salt

1 teaspoon of olive oil

Section 4

Multiple Uses.

Step 1

Finely chop all the dark chocolate and place into a heatproof bowl.

Step 2

On medium high heat add the non dairy milk and salt and bring to a low boil. Be careful not to over cook and burn.

Once boiled remove from heat and pour the non dairy milk over the dark chocolate and cover immediately with a plate. Give it a couple swirls to make sure the milk covers the chocolate completely and let sit for 4-5 minutes.

Step 3

Remove plate and begin to whisk the chocolate until smooth and glossy. *(Do not over mix)*. Now add the olive oil and whisk again.

Step 4

Allow it to thicken at room temperature before using.

Ingredients To Buy

Ingredients	Have It	Buy It
Dark chocolate without milk in it	☆	☐
I use 72% cocoa dark chocolate	☆	☐
Non dairy milk	☆	☐
Sea salt	☆	☐
Olive oil	☆	☐
	☆	☐
	☆	☐
	☆	☐
	☆	☐
	☆	☐
	☆	☐
	☆	☐
	☆	☐
	☆	☐

Section 5

Dill & Garlic Hummus

Ingredients

1 can of chick peas

2 cloves of chopped garlic

1/4 cup of chopped dill

1/4 cup of tahini (ground sesame seeds)

the juice of 1 lemon

1/4 cup of cold vegetable broth

1 teaspoon of cumin

1 tablespoon of sea salt

1 teaspoon of cracked pepper

Section 6

Hummus Happy

Step 1

Using a food processor add the can of chick peas and give it a few good pulses to start.

Now add the rest of the ingredients ***except*** the dill and vegetable stock.

Step 2

Turn your food processor on puree and slowly add the ***cold*** vegetable stock while it is pureeing. Once the hummus has reached a smooth consistency turn the processor off and scoop into a bowl.

Step 3

Now add the finely chopped dill to the hummus and give it a couple of stirs making sure the dill is mixed thoroughly.

Step 4

Scoop the hummus and put into a serving dish and top with a drizzle of olive oil and a few sprinkles of dill. Serve with fresh pitas or raw carrots and celery sticks.

Done!

Ingredients To Buy

Ingredients	Have It	Buy It
Chick peas	★	☐
Garlic cloves	★	☐
Fresh dill	★	☐
Tahini (Ground sesame seeds)	★	☐
Lemon	★	☐
Vegetable broth	★	☐
Cumin	★	☐
Sea salt teaspoon	★	☐
Cracked pepper	★	☐
	★	☐
	★	☐
	★	☐
	★	☐
	★	☐

Section 7

Gorilla Vegetable Zesty Dip & Dressing

Use This On Salads Or Vegetables For A Creamy Kick

Ingredients

1 cup sunflower oil

1/3 cup of soy milk

1 tablespoon sriracha sauce

1 tablespoon sea salt

1 teaspoon onion granules r

1 teaspoon of garlic powder

3 tablespoons of lemon juice

1/4 cup of chives

Section 8

It's The Best Zest

Step 1

Add the oil and milk together in a glass. Using your hand blender mix together until you have a thick creamy substance.

Step 2

Now add the remainder of the ingredients except for the chives and give it a mix again. Taste to see if you need a little more salt or lemon to your liking.

Step 3

Add in the chopped chives and give it a stir with a fork a few times and your done.

Gorilla Note: If you like it a little more spicy just add some more of the sriracha and give it a few more stirs.

Ingredients To Buy

Ingredients	Have It	Buy It
Sunflower oil	★	☐
Soy milk	★	☐
Sriracha sauce	★	☐
Sea salt	★	☐
Onion granules	★	☐
garlic powder	★	☐
lemon juice	★	☐
chives	★	☐
	★	☐
	★	☐
	★	☐
	★	☐
	★	☐
	★	☐
	★	☐

Section 9

Delicious Mushroom Gravy

This Is My Go Too Gravy. Super Easy To Make And Tastes Amazing .... I Promise!

Ingredients

2 cups of sliced mushrooms

2 cups of vegetable broth

2 tablespoons of soy sauce or tamari sauce

1 teaspoon of sea salt

1 teaspoon of cracked black pepper

2 tablespoons of olive oil

1 half of diced onion shallot

1 teaspoon of thyme

1 teaspoon of garlic powder

3 tablespoons of corn starch or flour

Section 10

Getting On The Gravy Train

Step 1

On medium high heat add the olive oil and chopped shallots. Cook until soft then add the chopped garlic and the mushrooms.

Let this cook for approximately 4-5 minutes until mushrooms are cooked.

Step 2

Add the vegetable broth and the remainder of the ingredients ***EXCEPT*** the corn starch. Allow the broth to come to a light boil for a few minutes then lower the heat.

Step 3

Now add the corn starch. Using a whisk mix well getting out any clumps that might try to form. Continue to stir until the gravy thickens.

Gorilla Note:

If you like a thicker gravy just add a bit more corn starch and stir. If you like a thinner grave just add a bit more vegetable broth.

Done!

Ingredients To Buy

Ingredients	Have It	Buy It
Mushrooms	★	☐
Vegetable broth	★	☐
Soy sauce or tamari	★	☐
Sea salt	★	☐
Cracked black pepper	★	☐
Olive oil	★	☐
Onion shallot	★	☐
Thyme	★	☐
Garlic powder	★	☐
Corn starch or flour	★	☐
	★	☐
	★	☐
	★	☐
	★	☐
	★	☐

Chapter 8

Easy Appetizers

Here are some super easy appetizers you can make if your entertaining. They are delicious and quick to make. Serve to the fussiest vegans you know. They will love you. It doesnt hurt to serve some adult drinks with them too ;)

Section 1

Cucumber Hummus Bites

These Are Great For Guests And Super Simple

Ingredients

Amounts vary with portions

1 large English cucumber

hummus (see sauces)

fresh dill

green pitted olives

smoked paprika

sea salt

Section 2

You Might Want To Make Extra

Step 1

Cut cucumber in I inch thick pieces *(leave skin on).*

Add a tablespoon of hummus and green olive on top of each piece of cucumber.

Sprinkle a little smoked paprika and a dash of sea salt.

Top with some fresh dill.

Step 2

Serve and enjoy!

Ingredients To Buy

Ingredients	Have It	Buy It
Large English cucumber	☆	☐
Hummus (See sauces)	☆	☐
Fresh dill	☆	☐
Green pitted olives	☆	☐
Smoked paprika	☆	☐
Sea salt	☆	☐
	☆	☐
	☆	☐
	☆	☐
	☆	☐
	☆	☐
	☆	☐
	☆	☐
	☆	☐

Section 3

Peppers and Hummus/Avocado Sliders

OMG! I Love These!

Ingredients

Amounts vary with portions

1 red pepper

1 yellow pepper

1 green pepper

1 cup of hummus *(see sauces)*

1-2 avocados

sea salt

cracked pepper

Section 4

Slide DiMaggio Slide>>>>>>>

Step 1

Slice each pepper length wise in I inch sections and clean out seeds and vein lining. *(each piece should have sides slightly curled)*

Step 2

Spread a generous amount of hummus in each pepper slice.

Step 3

Cut the avocado in even strips and place a piece below or on top of the hummus. Add a pinch of sea salt and cracked pepper.

Step 4

You can serve these right away or chill for an hour first for more texture.

Your Guests Will Love These!

Ingredients To Buy

Ingredients	Have It	Buy It
Red pepper	★	☐
Yellow pepper	★	☐
Green pepper	★	☐
Hummus (See sauces)	★	☐
Avocado	★	☐
Sea salt	★	☐
Cracked pepper	★	☐
	★	☐
	★	☐
	★	☐
	★	☐
	★	☐
	★	☐
	★	☐
	★	☐

Section 5

Italian Crusty Bread and Dipping Oil

What Sa Matter For You ?

Ingredients

2 cloves of garlic finely chopped

1 teaspoon of chili flakes

1 teaspoon of rosemary

1/2 teaspoon of thyme

6 tablespoons of a good olive oil

2 1/2 tablespoons of balsamic vinegar

1/2 teaspoon of sea salt

1/2 teaspoon of cracked pepper

1 loaf of crusty Italian bread

Section 6

Dipity Doo Da

Step 1

In a shallow bowl add the chopped garlic, Chile pepper flakes, rosemary, thyme, sea salt and pepper then mix it together.

Step 2

Now pour the olive oil directly over top of the mix and give a little stir to incorporate the flavors.

Step 3

Add the balsamic vinegar in the middle of the olive oil. Do not stir just let it settle on its own.

Step 4

Slice the bread into small pieces and plate around the bowl of dipping oil and serve.

Ingredients To Buy

Ingredients	Have It	Buy It
Garlic cloves	☆	☐
Chili flakes	☆	☐
Rosemary	☆	☐
Thyme	☆	☐
Olive oil	☆	☐
Balsamic vinegar	☆	☐
Sea salt	☆	☐
Cracked pepper	☆	☐
Loaf of crusty Italian bread	☆	☐
	☆	☐
	☆	☐
	☆	☐
	☆	☐
	☆	☐
	☆	☐

Section 7

Warm Stuffed Mushrooms

Served Warm People Are Going To Devour These!

Ingredients

15-20 button mushrooms

1 small onion

1 red pepper

1/4 cup of chopped walnuts

1 cup finely chopped spinach

1 tablespoon parsley

1 garlic clove chopped

1/2 cup bread crumbs

1/2 cup nutritional yeast

1 tablespoon of oregano & basil

1 tablespoon sea salt

1 tablespoon cracked pepper

3 tablespoons olive oil

Section 8

Good Stuff Stuffing

Step 1

Pre heat the oven to 350 degree F

Using a wet paper towel clean the mushrooms by giving them a good wipe. Now gently pull the stem out of each mushroom so that you have a small opening to the mushroom cap. Keep the mushroom stems and set aside.

Step 2

Now add to your food processor the mushroom stems, onions, red peppers, walnuts, spinach and pulse to create a small crumble. ***Do Not Puree***

Step 3

Place a frying pan on medium high heat and add the olive oil. Now add the crumble from the processor and the remainder of the ingredients. Cook until you get a little crust and browning to begin. Then Remove from heat.

Step 4

Using a small spoon start to stuff the inside of each mushroom cap with the ingredients. Place them on an oven pan facing up and bake for approximately 20 minutes. Done.

Ingredients To Buy

Ingredients	Have It	Buy It
Button mushrooms	★	☐
Onion	★	☐
Red pepper	★	☐
Walnuts	★	☐
Spinach	★	☐
Parsley garlic	★	☐
Bread crumbs	★	☐
Nutritional yeast	★	☐
Oregano	★	☐
Basil	★	☐
Sea salt	★	☐
Cracked pepper	★	☐
Olive oil	★	☐
	★	☐
	★	☐

Section 9

Warm Spinach And Artichoke Dip

No Joke Artichoke .... This Is Creamy And Delicious!

Ingredients

1 block of firm tofu

1 medium size shallot or onion

4 cups of fresh spinach

1 cup of artichoke

2 cloves of minced garlic

2 tablespoons of lemon

1/2 cup of nutritional yeast

1 tablespoon of chili flakes

1 tablespoon of onion powder

1 tablespoon of sea salt

1 tablespoon of cracked pepper

2 tablespoons of olive oil

Section 10

No Double Dipping :)

Step 1 Preheat oven to 350 degree F

On medium high heat add 2 tablespoons of olive oil to a frying pan and add the chopped shallots. Once they become translucent turn the heat to medium low then add the chopped garlic and spinach. Cook until the spinach wilts then turn off heat and set aside.

Step 2

In your food processor add the tofu, lemon, nutritional yeast, chili flakes, onion powder, salt and pepper. Then puree for about 20 seconds and stop.

Step 3

Now add the onions, garlic, wilted spinach and artichokes to the food processor and pulse several times 10-20 *(depending on your processor power)* to chop the artichokes and help mix the final dish. *(again do not over mix or puree)*

Step 4

Now bake in the oven for approximately 25 minutes until the top begins to brown.

Serve with Fresh Pitas and or Nachos! Tummy!

Ingredients To Buy

Ingredients	Have It	Buy It
Block of firm tofu	★	☐
Shallot or onion	★	☐
Spinach	★	☐
Artichoke	★	☐
Garlic cloves	★	☐
Lemon	★	☐
Nutritional yeast	★	☐
Chili flakes	★	☐
Onion powder	★	☐
Sea salt	★	☐
Cracked pepper	★	☐
Olive oil	★	☐
	★	☐
	★	☐
	★	☐

Conclusion

Just a final note to thank you very much for buying my Vegan cook book.

I hope you enjoyed some of or all the creations in this book. If they didn't turn out just right the first time that's ok. Sometimes it takes a few tries to tweak things to your own style and flavors.

I am always working on new tastes, textures and flavors and already started writing another vegan cook book with more advanced techniques and creativity.

I wish you all a happy, healthy and wealthy life and may you be blessed with good food, good friends and good times.

Much Luv

The Vegan Gorilla
Namaste

CPSIA information can be obtained
at www.ICGtesting.com
Printed in the USA
LVHW060412301018
595302LV00004B/142/P